Volcanos & Earthquakes

Andres Llamas Ruiz

Illustrations by Ali Garoussi

Sterling Publishing Co., Inc.

New York

Illustrations by Ali Garoussi
Text by Andrés Llamas Ruiz
Translated by Natalia Tizón

Library of Congress Cataloging-in-Publication Data

Llamas Ruiz, Andrés.
   [Volcanes y terremotos. English]
   Volcanos and earthquakes / by Andres Llamas Ruiz ;
illustrations by Ali Garoussi.
        p.   cm. — (Sequences of earth & space)
   Includes index.
   Summary: Describes the origins and effects of volcanoes and
earthquakes, including tsunamis and volcanic islands.
   ISBN 0-8069-9745-1
   1. Volcanoes—Juvenile literature.   2. Earthquakes—Juvenile
literature. [1. Volcanoes.   2. Earthquakes.]   I. Garoussi, Ali,
ill.   II. Title.   III. Series: Llamas Ruiz, Andrés.   Secuencias de
la tierra y el espacio.   English.
QE521.3.L5713   1997
551.21—dc21   96–37981
                                       CIP
                                        AC

1   3   5   7   9   10   8   6   4   2

Published by Sterling Publishing Company, Inc.
387 Park Avenue South, New York, N.Y. 10016
Originally published in Spain by Ediciones Estes
©1996 by Ediciones Lema, S.L.
English version and translation © 1997 by Sterling Publishing Company, Inc.
Distributed in Canada by Sterling Publishing
℅ Canadian Manda Group, One Atlantic Avenue, Suite 105
Toronto, Ontario, Canada M6K 3E7
Distributed in Great Britain and Europe by Cassell PLC
Wellington House, 125 Strand, London WC2R 0BB, England
Distributed in Australia by Capricorn Link (Australia) Pty Ltd.
P.O. Box 6651, Baulkham Hills, Business Centre, NSW 2153, Australia
Printed and Bound in Spain

Sterling ISBN 0-8069-9745-1

Table of Contents

The Inside of the Earth

Scientists believe that the inside structure of the earth has been the same for the past 4 billion years.

Our planet is made up of several layers. The exterior one is the crust, the hard layer on which we live. The mantle—a layer of warmer, heavier rock on which the crust rests—lies just beneath it. Parts of the mantle are viscous, flowing with "convection movements." Beneath the mantle is the metallic core of the earth, which reads millions of degrees in temperature. The core itself consists of two parts: the liquid external core (formed by liquid iron and nickel) and the solid inner core (made of what geologists think is a solid, warm iron sphere).

Seismic activity (earthquakes) and volcanic eruptions are the result of the planet's internal activity.

1. The crust is a solid, thin, relatively cold layer.

2. At a depth of 124 miles, the earth's temperature reaches 2732°F and the rock is white hot.

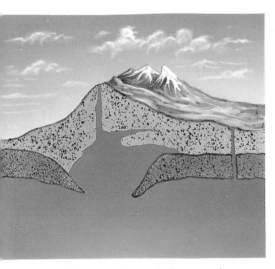

During a volcanic eruption, material that rises from the mantle is called lava (molten rock). It emerges abruptly and forms curtains of fire.

Forces that run through the mantle may influence the earth's crust to cause the formation of huge mountains.

3. Molten matter expelled during a volcanic eruption comes from the top part of the mantle.

4. This molten matter is called magma.

5. Movement of the outer core's metallic liquid, which conducts electricity, creates the earth's magnetic field.

Continents Move

Today, there are seven large land masses called continents. However, 200 million years ago, these continents were all one huge block of land, now known as the "Pangaea" supercontinent. This mass ultimately broke into several pieces that separated and formed continents.

Have you ever noticed that the shape of the African and South American coasts match each other? In 1912, the scientist Alfred Wegener also noticed this. He stated that continents move because they rest on the tectonic plates that form the earth's crust. This motion is called continental drift and is created by convection movement in the mantle. The plates move because of the streams of viscous rock that flow through the mantle. Some plates drag oceans while others drag continents.

The earth's crust is formed by at least eighteen tectonic plates, although there are six large ones.

1. The plates can move at a speed of up to 4 inches per year (although they average only 1 inch annually). They glide over a layer of softer rock called the asthenosphere.

2. When the plates move, their edges separate or collide to cause earthquakes.

3. Tectonic plates have three types of boundaries:

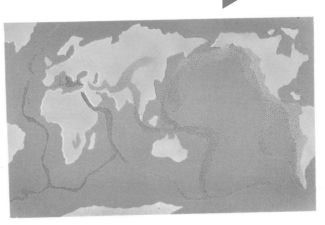

Zones of seismic activity and volcanos are closely related to the points of the crust where two tectonic plates meet.

The movement of the continents relative to one another is called continental drift. As you see here, the earth's exterior appearance has changed greatly over millions of years.

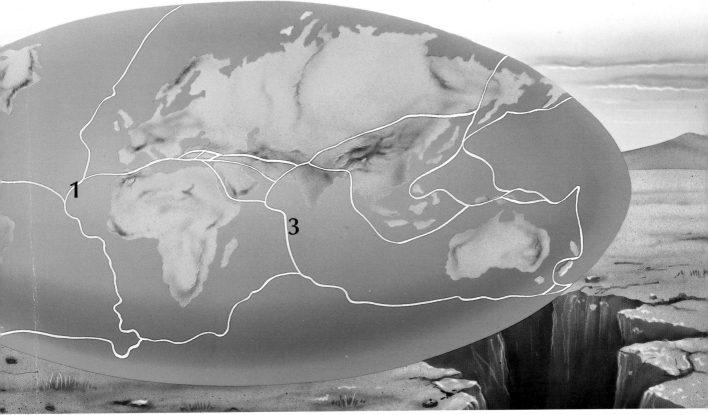

(a) divergent boundaries, which separate from each other; as the plates pull apart, magma emerges from the earth's lower layers to form a new ocean bottom.

(b) convergent boundaries, formed when two plates meet in a frontal collision or one slides over the other.

(c) transform or sliding boundaries that are caused by sideways slippage of the plates.

Plates Collide

Tectonic plates move a few inches every year, either approaching or separating from one another. When matter from the earth's mantle flows up, propelled by convection movement, it causes a split in the earth's crust that pushes the tectonic plates in opposite directions and produces oceanic ridges. This is how oceans develop. Every year, for example, as North America and Europe slowly separate, molten rock at the bottom of the Atlantic Ocean forms new ground to fill in the void between the plates that move those continents.

In many places around the world, the ocean floor sinks into the mantle. These areas are called subduction zones. A subduction zone runs the length of the west coast of the United States.

When two plates meet, one may slide over the other to cause great stress on the rock below the earth's crust. This stress may create ruptures or faults between the rocks. This is how earthquakes start!

Basaltic magma rises from the asthenosphere to the ocean's floor along mid-oceanic ridges. When cold water from the ocean comes in contact with magma, it solidifies and becomes the new ocean floor.

1. Downward movement drags the plates toward the mantle to create subduction zones and oceanic trenches.

When water rich in metallic sulfides from the earth's mantle meets the cold ocean water, the sulfides harden to form "chimneys" that surround the opening of the black fumaroles, or black smokers, which are holes in the ocean floor that emit hot gases and vapors.

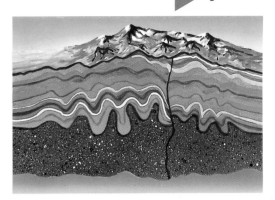

When tectonic plates collide, they pleat like an accordion to create mountain ranges and cause earthquakes.

2. At the same time, the lithosphere (the rigid crust and upper mantle that flows on the top of the soft asthenosphere) is consumed when it reaches the lower depths of the mantle.

3. A coastal volcanic mountain range is formed when a plate that supports an ocean sinks under a plate that supports a continent.

Seismic Waves

Most earthquakes occur at the specific areas of the earth's surface where the tectonic plates meet. When there is an earthquake, the seismic disturbances generate mechanical vibrations in the shape of waves that either move upward, toward the surface, or downward, toward the earth's core. These mechanical vibrations cause catastrophes on the earth's surface! The waves can be detected by seismographs and can be of three different types: compressional waves (P, or primary waves, which run lengthwise), shear waves (S, or secondary waves, which move from side to side), or surface waves (which move in all directions and create the most structural damage and transmit most of the energy; they are also called Rayleigh and Love waves).

An earthquake's point of origin (the place in the fault where a rupture starts) is called the focus of the earthquake. Although the focus can be as much as 430 miles deep, it usually goes down only 60 miles or less. Earthquakes with shallow focuses often cause the most damage! The point on the earth's surface directly above the focus is called the epicenter.

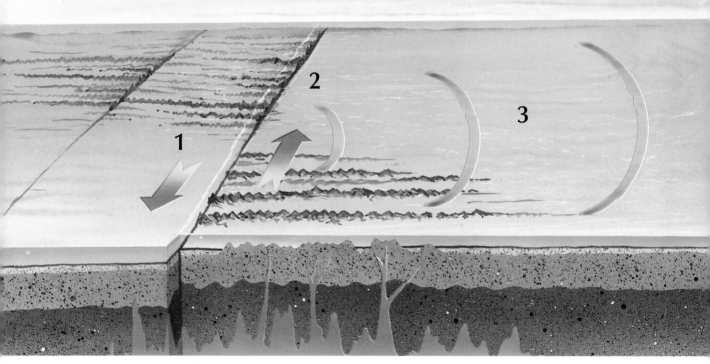

Earthquakes are caused by rock masses sliding along the faults.

1. Rocks have elastic properties and so deformation energy accumulates.

2. When the deformation strain becomes greater than the frictional force, the fault ruptures at its weakest point.

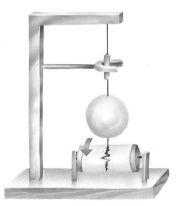

Seismographs detect and measure the collisions before an earthquake. By comparing the measurements of the seismographs placed in several places, experts can locate an earthquake's point of origin.

During an earthquake vibrations spread in different ways:
A. Primary waves are the fastest-moving waves; they can travel through the earth in 20 minutes.
B. Secondary waves travel through the earth's mantle.
C. Love waves.
D. Rayleigh waves.

A

B

C

D

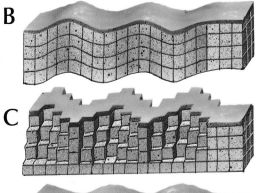

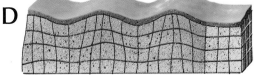

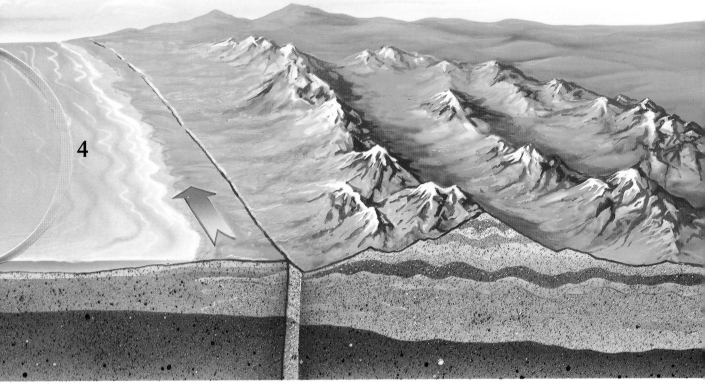

4

3. Then, the energy that was stored is released in the form of seismic waves that spread in all directions from the focus of the earthquake.

4. This rupture can last several seconds or even minutes, depending on the size of the earthquake.

The Earth Shakes

Each year there are more than half a million earthquakes measured, but fewer than one thousand of them cause serious damage. Most are so weak that people do not even feel them.

Earthquakes originate in the areas where adjacent rocks are stressed by opposing directional forces. When the strain becomes greater than the resistance of the rock, the rock breaks along a plane to form a fault. During this rupture, rocks travel quickly because they release the stress they were under. Then, seismic energy creates a train of waves that move from the point of origin or focus to the surface of the earth. The earth begins to shake and huge cracks appear in the ground.

There are different scales to measure the intensity of an earthquake. The Richter scale measures the movement of the ground from 0 to 9. It is a logarithmic scale, which means that each number represents an intensity ten times greater than the previous number. The highest-magnitude earthquake ever detected registered 8.9 degrees on the Richter scale.

The Mercalli scale measures the intensity of earthquakes by rating damage caused from I (not noticeable to people) to XII (total destruction).

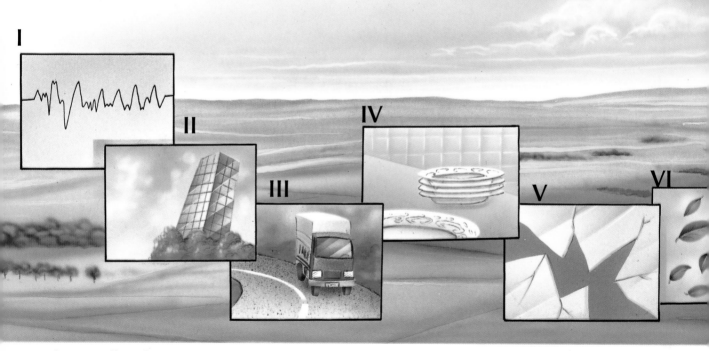

The Mercalli scale:
- **I.** Detected by seismographs and very sensitive people.
- **II.** Big buildings move slightly.
- **III.** Similar vibrations to those of a truck passing by.
- **IV.** Dishes, windows, etc., vibrate.
- **V.** Objects may fall and break; nearly everyone feels it.
- **VI.** Heavy furniture moves, trees shake, windows break.

One kind of special seismograph indicated the direction of an earthquake. Where the ball falls shows the direction of the focus of the seismic activity.

The earth's inner core absorbs and detours primary and secondary seismic waves to create "shadow areas" where the waves do not reach.

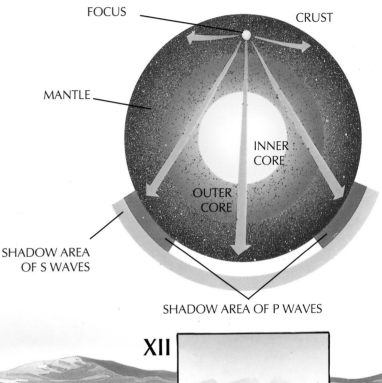

FOCUS

CRUST

MANTLE

INNER CORE

OUTER CORE

SHADOW AREA OF S WAVES

SHADOW AREA OF P WAVES

VII. Damage to poorly constructed buildings.

VIII. Slight damage to well-constructed buildings.

IX. Underground pipes break and there are cracks in the ground.

X. Railway tracks bend; landslides.

XI. Bridges are destroyed.

XII. Total destruction of buildings.

Big Earthquakes

The force of energy released in a big earthquake is truly awe-inspiring. In inhabited areas, it can create real catastrophes with thousands of casualties. The effects of an earthquake are often worsened by other factors, such as landslides and changes in the earth's surface caused by the plates colliding with or sliding over each other. Frictional movement along the faults causes further damage.

In some areas, rock and snow avalanches can move at speeds of more than 170 miles per hour.

4

Depending on the characteristics of the region where the earthquake occurs, consequences may vary:

1. Superficial ruptures.
2. Ground vibrations are strongest near the fault and less intense as they move farther away.

If an earthquake is very strong, nearby cities may be completely destroyed. Buildings and infrastructure collapse and seismic activity causes a large number of fires.

California's impressive San Andreas sliding fault is more than 620 miles long.

3

2

1

3. In mountainous areas, there may be dangerous landslides and avalanches.

4. Coastal areas may be affected by destructive floods.

Tsunami Waves

When there is a big earthquake or a volcanic eruption under the sea, water from the ocean bottom surges upward. What happens then? A wave forms that moves at high speeds along the surface until it reaches the shore, where it becomes a killer wave known as a tsunami. These seismic waves travel at more than 500 miles per hour, increasing in height (from less than 3 feet or so) to finally become a vast wall of water sometimes more than 100 feet tall as it hits the coastline. Although there have been some tsunamis in the Atlantic Ocean, most occur in the Pacific.

The effects of tsunamis on coastal towns are catastrophic. These waves are sometimes responsible for more deaths than any other phenomena related with earthquakes or volcanos.

A tsunami can travel more than 1000 miles across the sea before reaching the shore. Between 1 minute and 1 hour can go by between two waves.

In lakes, ponds, and dams, waves from distant earthquakes can cause waves known as "seiches."

4

1. An undersea earthquake or volcanic explosion causes a great vertical motion of water.

2. A wave-like movement reaches the surface.

3. The waves move along the surface at great speed.

4. As they approach the coast, where the water is shallower, the waves reduce in speed, but increase in size.

A Volcano Is Formed

A volcano is a "mountain of fire" through which material from inside the earth is expelled. In ancient times, people thought volcanos were the houses of some of the gods. Today, we think volcanos form in areas where the earth's crust is weak.

Most volcanic eruptions occur in areas where the tectonic plates meet. During an eruption, molten underground rock (magma) and hot gases force their way out to the surface through holes and cracks in the earth's crust. Magma expelled by volcanos is formed at a location of 30–150 miles underground, where rock temperatures are very high and very close to their melting point.

Volcanic eruptions are caused by magma rising to the earth's surface through a system of "feeder pipes" up to 150 miles deep, which connect the liquid magma with the earth's crust.

1. A cone formed by alternating layers of lava and ash.

Undersea volcanic eruptions are especially violent because the magma explodes when it cools down as it comes in contact with the water. If the volcano's cone emerges from the water, it will be destroyed by the waves and its materials will be dispersed.

Pressure forces hot water through black fumaroles or smokers, which are chimneys formed of metallic sulfides.

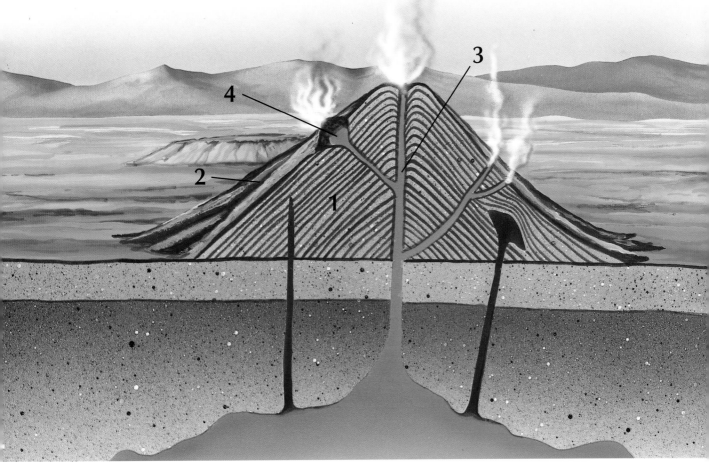

2. The cone is reinforced by solidified layers of lava.

3. Normally, the central crater becomes larger when the magma holding the walls of the crater recedes back inside the chimney.

4. The magma that flows down the sides forms new craters, domes, and fissure lava flows.

Inactive Volcanos

Not all volcanos erupt. Some are extinguished after erupting once or twice, and some are "dormant," with a solid mass of lava clogging the exit. However, even dormant volcanos can pose a threat. Sometimes, they accumulate hot gases for hundreds of years. Finally, they reach a point where the pressure of the gases is so great it unclogs the top of the volcano to produce a powerful eruption that takes us by surprise.

Active volcanos are not dispersed randomly around our planet. They can be found in areas called "hot spots," which are located along the subduction zones (areas where the edge of one tectonic plate slides below the edge of another) and along the oceanic ridges.

A dormant volcano can go for many centuries without any noticeable signs of activity. Its top can be covered with snow, its sides covered with trees. Nothing indicates that it might erupt again. However, the top of the volcano can suddenly unclog and erupt.

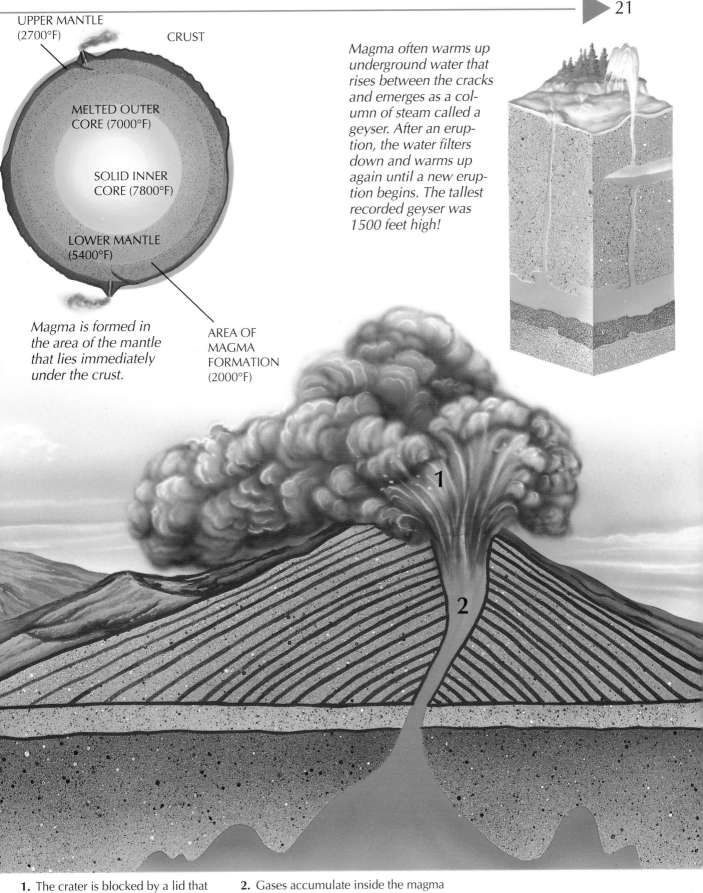

UPPER MANTLE
(2700°F)

CRUST

MELTED OUTER
CORE (7000°F)

SOLID INNER
CORE (7800°F)

LOWER MANTLE
(5400°F)

*Magma is formed in
the area of the mantle
that lies immediately
under the crust.*

AREA OF
MAGMA
FORMATION
(2000°F)

*Magma often warms up
underground water that
rises between the cracks
and emerges as a col-
umn of steam called a
geyser. After an erup-
tion, the water filters
down and warms up
again until a new erup-
tion begins. The tallest
recorded geyser was
1500 feet high!*

1

2

1. The crater is blocked by a lid that
looks "permanent" and consists of
solidified lava.

2. Gases accumulate inside the magma
chamber until they reach a point
where any small change can cause
an explosion.

The Eruption Starts

Many factors influence the way a volcano erupts.

Each volcano erupts in a different way, depending on the water and silica content of the magma. Silica-rich magmas are more viscous, so they trap more gas. When they erupt, they are more explosive.

Volcanic behavior varies, depending on age. Many volcanos release molten lava when they are young and erupt explosively when they grow old.

The form and size of the volcano's chimney also influence the eruption. If the chimney is very long and narrow, gases will be expelled at high speeds to reach great heights.

Once an eruption starts, a chain reaction will force it to continue without interruption until it reaches deeper levels of the magma chamber, where there is less gas and the viscosity is higher.

4

During an eruption, magma usually flows out to the surface through a vertical tube, although *some volcanos have side chimneys.*

1. When magma begins to rise, gases (steam, carbon dioxide, sulfur dioxide, hydrogen, and chlorine) may escape from the molten rock.

Volcanic explosions release an enormous amount of energy. The energy released by the 1980 explosion of Washington's Mount St. Helens destroyed all the trees in a 230-square-mile area.

Eruptions differ, depending on the water vapor and silica content in the magma.

A. A small amount of water vapor and silica produces quiet eruptions.

B. Less silica and a great deal of water vapor produces streams of fire that can be hundreds of feet tall.

C. Less water vapor and a great deal of silica creates a thick lava, which forms a dome that becomes progressively larger.

D. A great deal of both water vapor and silica produces violent explosions.

A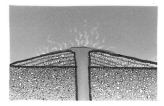

B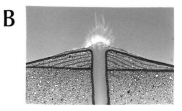

C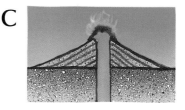

D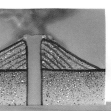

3

2

1

2. Pressure accumulates under the lava blocking the exit.

3. The higher the pressure inside the volcano, the greater the eruption will be.

4. If the lid pops off, the gases and liquid are expelled and spread as an explosion.

Types of Volcanos

It is very difficult to classify volcanos, since each can erupt in different ways and even change its behavior during the same eruption. There are some simple ways to think about volcanic eruptions: Some are explosive, some are medium, and some are quiet.

"Explosive" eruptions are characterized by thick lava that contains lots of gas. The sudden eruption forms a cinder cone built of pieces of volcanic rock and ash. Burning gas rises to the surface through an opening at the top of the volcano called a crater. Hot ash and rocks shoot into the air and pieces of molten rock (lava) are expelled like bombs, sometimes traveling long distances. In "quiet" eruptions, thick lava flows softly through cracks and holes, building steep-sided volcanic domes.

There are many intermediate cases, however. During a "medium" eruption, violent ash and gas explosions alternate with periods when thick lava flows gently down the side of the volcano. This is called a composite volcano.

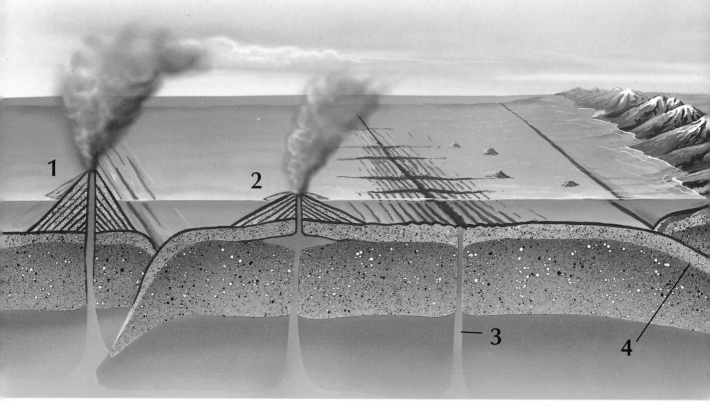

1. Volcanic mountain ranges of island arcs.

2. Thermal-vent volcanos that are created by the rising of very hot materials.

3. In the mid-oceanic ridges, magma rises through a system of underground fissures.

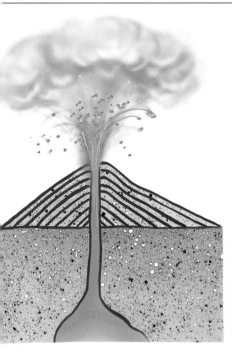
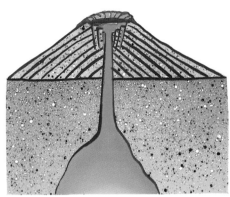
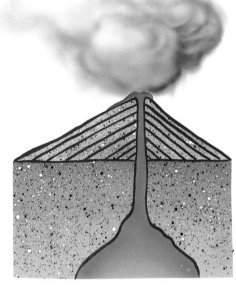

Types of eruptions:
Explosive volcano (cinder cone volcano).

Quiet volcano (composite volcano).

Medium-type volcano (lava dome volcano).

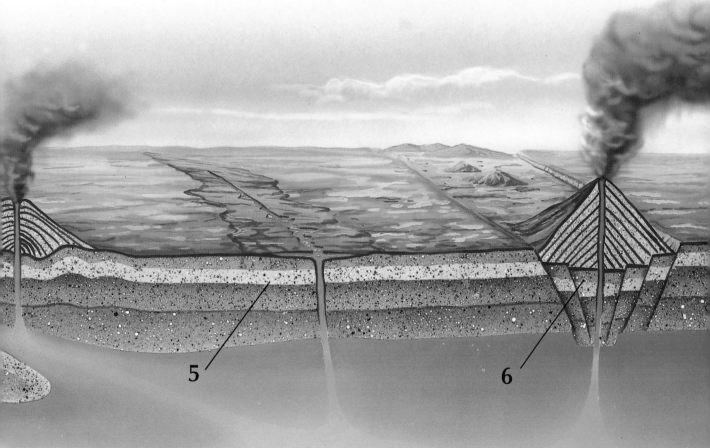

4. In subduction zones, the ocean plate sinks under the continental plate to form a volcanic mountain range.

5. In continental basalt-fissure lava flows, magma flows through fields of fissures that are hundreds of miles long.

6. In continental-drift volcanos, a continental plate splits in two and magma rises up through the faults.

Rivers of Lava

During an eruption, most magma is dispersed in the form of molten lava, which hardens and forms igneous rock. The most abundant of this type of rock is basalt, which appears in many areas on the ocean floor where lava hardened quickly as it came in contact with water. Most continents are also covered by a layer of basalt that can be many miles thick in some areas.

In quiet volcanos, great streams of molten lava flow gently through the cracks in the volcano. In this type of eruption, there are no catastrophic explosions.

When the lava is high in viscosity, it hardens quickly to pile up like a tower. This is called a volcanic dome. The more fluid the lava, the farther it can travel before hardening. In its most fluid state, it can travel many miles without anything stopping it.

The travel speed of the lava river depends on the terrain and the viscosity of the lava.

1. Even if the incline is insignificant, some lava flows can travel 120 miles.

2. Lava has a temperature close to 1000–2500°F, which makes it burn almost everything in its path.

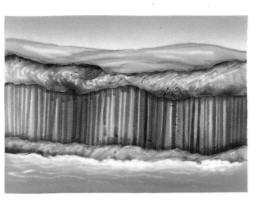

When the balsaltic magma cools down, it may contract and rupture to form spectacular columns that resemble artificial pillars.

The Giant's Causeway in Northern Ireland is a very special place formed by basaltic columns that are up to 20 feet high. Each column is 1 to 2 feet wide and has three to nine sides.

Some volcanos shoot hot ash and rocks into the air. Lava is expelled like bombs.

2

3

3. When an eruption stops, the landscape is covered by a black coat of hard lava. The lava may still flow intermittently through underground "lava rivers."

Dreaded Glowing Clouds

When there is an explosive eruption, a cloud of hot gases and fine ash can emerge from the volcano at temperatures ranging between 400°F and 1800°F.

This cloud, called glowing cloud, spreads quickly, sweeping the sides of the volcano in lava flows that travel faster than 60 miles per hour.

When the explosion goes straight up, the cloud can reach heights of more than 6 miles.

Sometimes an explosion only partially destroys the volcano's crater, propelling the cloud sideways. A quickly advancing wave of gas precedes the cloud, destroying just about everything in its path.

Glowing clouds are formed by volcanic gases and ash that fall down the sides of the volcano. In the 1902 explosion of Mt. Pelée volcano on the Caribbean island of Martinique, the cloud that was formed caused the death of thirty thousand inhabitants in the nearest town. There was only one survivor!

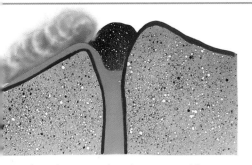

The glowing cloud is caused by a side eruption of volcanic material because there is a lid of solidified lava clogging the main opening.

*Inside a magma chamber, the heaviest minerals (**A**) settle at the bottom, while the lightest ones (**B**), such as quartz, rise to the ceiling.*

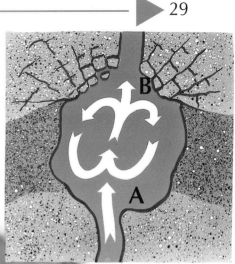

1. Inside the crater, the high pressure of the expanding gases aerates the magma.

2. An emulsion of gases, glass, and pieces of lava is formed. This cloud can rise to great heights.

3. The glowing cloud sweeps the side of the volcano at a speed of up to 60 miles per hour.

Volcanic Islands

Many islands are of volcanic origin. They are volcanos that rose from the bottom of the sea as molten rock emerged along mid-oceanic ridges—cracks in the crust where two plates were separating from each other.

Other volcanic islands are formed when one plate slides over another, causing the edge of the plate below to sink into the earth's mantle and melt. Molten rock from the crust, which is lighter and warmer than the rocks in the mantle, floats on the mantle and emerges from the ocean to create new volcanic islands that often form curved chains called island arc.

In time, volcanic islands are pushed down as the level of the ocean rises or as the sea bed sinks. Around islands set in warm, clear waters, coral grows so quickly on a sinking island that it forms an atoll (an island consisting of a reef surrounding a lagoon). More often, however, the islands simply disappear because of erosion caused by waves.

Some volcanos have exploded in such an impressive manner that there are only some pieces from the base of the crater left. In 1883, the eruption of Krakatoa (an island west of Java, in Indonesia) was heard 3000 miles away; its tsunamis caused the death of more than 36,000 people on a nearby island.

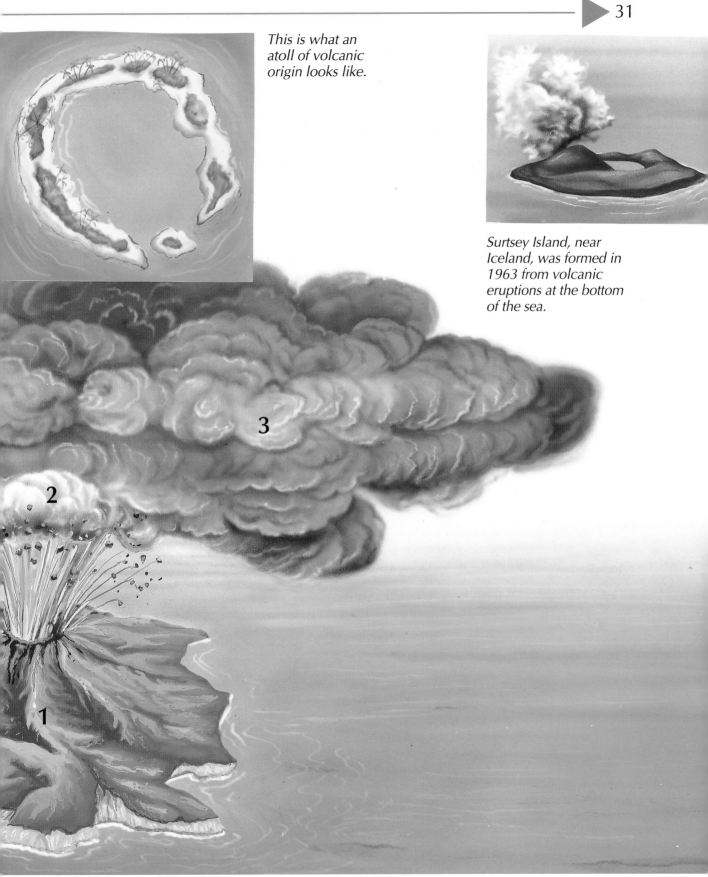

This is what an atoll of volcanic origin looks like.

Surtsey Island, near Iceland, was formed in 1963 from volcanic eruptions at the bottom of the sea.

1. The entire island exploded.

2. A column of rock and fire rose up to 2500 feet high.

3. The volcano projected 2 cubic miles of ash into the atmosphere.

Glossary

Basalt: Volcanic rock characteristic of ocean crust that is created by the solidification of molten lava from the upper mantle when it reaches cold ocean waters. It is the most common type of lava on the planet.

Crust: The thin outer layer of the earth, above which are the continents and oceans.

Epicenter: The point on the earth's surface that is the closest to the focus of an earthquake.

Fault: A crack or break in rock along which one side has moved relative to the other.

Geyser: Underground hot-water spring that, at more or less regular intervals, emits hot water and steam through cracks in the earth.

Lava: Magma that is expelled by an erupting volcano.

Magma: Hot molten rock that comes from the interior of the earth.

Magma chamber: A space 3 to 6 miles under the top of a volcano in which magma concentrates and where it undergoes physical and chemical transformations.

Seismic activity: An earthquake.

Silica: A combination of silicon and oxygen. This is the most important substance of the mineral kingdom because it is very abundant both in its free and combined state, such as quartz and flint.

Volcanic dome: A steep hill built of very viscous lava created as a result of volcanic activity.

Index